ADHD Solution Deck

Practical Strategies for Navigating Life wih Focus and Confidence

Charlice Evra

The author, publisher, distributor of this book has provided it with the intent of education only. The author is free from any damage, monetary loss, or otherwise to the read due to the information contained in this book.

Legal Notice

This book is under copyright. It is for your personal use and all commercial application is forbidden. You cannot sell, distribute, cut, quote, paraphrase or amend any part of it without the express permission of the author or publisher.

Disclaimer Notice

I write this book to help my readers improve their quality of life and find lasting solutions to mental health disorders. The content in the book is properly researched and fact-based with anecdotal evidence on the symptoms of the condition and the way to find solution to it. The information in this book shouldn't be used and isn't a substitute for medical advice and treatment. It cannot and shouldn't replace your healthcare provider or doctor.

Contents

Introduction

Attention Deficit Hyperactivity Disorder (ADHD) is a neurodevelopmental disorder characterized by persistent patterns of *inattention*, *hyperactivity*, and *impulsivity* that interfere with daily functioning. It affects individuals across the lifespan, from childhood through adulthood.

Attention Deficit Hyperactivity Disorder (ADHD) is among the most prevalent neurodevelopmental disorders globally, affecting approximately 5-7% of children. This prevalence translates to millions of individuals worldwide grappling with its challenges.

While ADHD is commonly associated with childhood, it's crucial to recognize that its impact extends beyond youth. Many individuals continue to experience ADHD symptoms well into adolescence and adulthood, necessitating ongoing support and management strategies throughout the lifespan.

Research indicates variations in ADHD prevalence rates across different populations and cultures, suggesting that both genetic and environmental factors contribute to its development.

Neurobiological Basis

Research has shed light on the neurobiological underpinnings of ADHD, highlighting alterations in brain structure and function that contribute to its symptomatology.

Key areas of the brain implicated in ADHD include the **prefrontal cortex, striatum, and cerebellum,** which play crucial roles in attention, impulse control, and executive functioning.

Structural imaging studies have revealed differences in brain volume and connectivity patterns in individuals with ADHD compared to neurotypical individuals. Functional imaging studies have also identified aberrant activity in brain regions responsible for regulating attention, inhibiting impulses, and coordinating motor function.

Dysregulation of neurotransmitters, particularly **dopamine and norepinephrine**, is thought to play a central role in ADHD. These neurotransmitters modulate various cognitive and behavioral functions, including attention, motivation, and reward processing.

Dysfunction in dopaminergic and noradrenergic pathways disrupts neural communication, contributing to the hallmark symptoms of ADHD, such as inattention, hyperactivity, and impulsivity.

Co-occurring Conditions

ADHD rarely exists in isolation; it frequently coexists with other mental health disorders, such as anxiety, depression, and learning disabilities.

These co-occurring conditions can exacerbate ADHD symptoms and complicate treatment planning, necessitating a comprehensive approach to assessment and intervention.

Anxiety disorders are among the most prevalent co-occurring conditions in individuals with ADHD, characterized by excessive worry, fear, and avoidance behaviors.

The interplay between ADHD and anxiety can heighten emotional dysregulation, impair attentional control, and interfere with adaptive functioning.

Depressive symptoms are also common among individuals with ADHD, contributing to feelings of sadness, hopelessness, and low self-esteem. The presence of comorbid depression can exacerbate impairments in motivation, energy levels, and social engagement, further compromising overall functioning and quality of life.

Learning disabilities, such as dyslexia and dyscalculia, frequently co-occur with ADHD, presenting additional challenges in academic settings.

Difficulties in reading, writing, and mathematical reasoning can compound the academic struggles associated with ADHD, necessitating specialized educational interventions and accommodations.

Impact on Daily Life

ADHD can exert a profound impact on various aspects of daily life, influencing academic and occupational performance, social relationships, and emotional well-being. You may face challenges in *organization, time management, task completion, and emotional regulation,* which can hinder your ability to meet responsibilities and achieve goals.

In educational settings, ADHD symptoms may manifest as difficulties in focusing on tasks, staying organized, and completing assignments on time. Academic performance may suffer, leading to frustration, low self-esteem, and academic underachievement. Similarly, in the workplace, ADHD-related impairments may affect your productivity, interpersonal relationships, and job satisfaction, potentially jeopardizing career advancement and stability.

Socially, you may also struggle with impulsivity, social inhibition, and difficulties in understanding social cues, making it challenging to establish and maintain relationships. You may experience feelings of isolation, rejection, and inadequacy, further exacerbating emotional distress and psychological well-being.

Emotional regulation difficulties are common among those suffering from ADHD, leading to mood swings, irritability, and heightened reactivity to stressors. Coping with intense emotions can be overwhelming, affecting quality of life and interpersonal functioning.

The good news is that you may not suffer many of these symptoms, as I've discovered in my own personal experience. While I had to work harder than others to maintain relationships, get things done, and maintain excellent academic standards, life has been good generally. I did well in my university, got a good business going, and consistently maintain my relationships. I know I was inhibit to some extent, due to my ADHD, but when life gives you lemons, *you make LEMONADE.*

Diagnostic Criteria

The diagnosis of ADHD is based on specific criteria outlined in the Diagnostic and Statistical Manual of Mental Disorders (DSM-5), a standardized classification system used by healthcare professionals worldwide.

To receive a diagnosis of ADHD, you must exhibit persistent patterns of inattention, hyperactivity, and impulsivity that significantly impair functioning across multiple settings, such as school, work, and social interactions.

Diagnostic assessment for ADHD typically involves comprehensive evaluation by healthcare professionals, including physicians, psychologists, or psychiatrists.

This evaluation may include clinical interviews, behavior rating scales, observation of behavior in various settings, and consideration of medical and developmental history. Accurate diagnosis is essential for guiding treatment decisions and developing personalized interventions.

The DSM-5 outlines criteria for three subtypes of ADHD: predominantly inattentive presentation, predominantly hyperactive-impulsive presentation, and combined presentation.

Each subtype presents unique challenges and may require tailored interventions to address predominant symptoms effectively. Before going further into this book and learning strategies to manage your symptoms, you first need to know which subtype of ADHD you're suffering from.

Why this classification?

Well, ADHD is not a one-size-fits-all condition; it manifests in diverse ways, leading to the classification of three primary subtypes based on predominant symptom presentation. Let's look at each of these types in order:

Predominantly Inattentive Presentation: Individuals with this subtype primarily struggle with inattention, often appearing forgetful, disorganized, and easily distracted. They may have difficulty sustaining attention on tasks, following through on instructions, and organizing their thoughts and belongings. I've learnt that I fall into this group myself, which seems to be the simplest of all. It is also these group I'm writing this book for because the other two may require professional intervention and rigorous diagnosis, which a mere book cannot provide.

Predominantly Hyperactive-Impulsive Presentation: This subtype is characterized by excessive motor activity and impulsivity. Individuals may appear restless, fidgety, and prone to acting without forethought. They may struggle with impulse control, interrupting others, and engaging in risky behaviors.

Combined Presentation: This subtype involves a combination of inattentive, hyperactive, and impulsive symptoms, reflecting a broad range of challenges across multiple domains of functioning. Individuals with the combined presentation often experience the most significant impairments and may require comprehensive interventions targeting various symptom domains.

Identifying the specific subtype of ADHD is critical for tailoring interventions to address the predominant symptoms effectively.

Carefully observe your symptoms and behavioral trait to understand what subtype your ADHD falls into. If you have decided that it is the first subtype you're suffering from, then the strategies in this book can help you manage the symptoms.

However, if you're experiencing the last two, you should be ready to see a health professional. That doesn't mean you can't use this book at all. Rather, use it alone with your medication, but not alone.

Lifespan Implications

As mentioned previously, ADHD is not simply a childhood disorder; its impact *extends across the lifespan*, influencing various aspects of development, functioning, and well-being.

While ADHD symptoms may evolve over time, the challenges associated with the disorder can persist into adolescence and adulthood, necessitating ongoing support and management strategies.

In childhood, ADHD symptoms often manifest as difficulties in attention, impulse control, and hyperactivity, impacting academic performance, social relationships, and self-esteem. Early intervention is crucial for minimizing the long-term consequences of ADHD and promoting optimal developmental outcomes.

As individuals with ADHD transition into adolescence, they may face unique challenges related to academic demands, peer relationships, and identity formation. Impulsivity, risk-taking behaviors, and difficulties in self-regulation can increase the risk of academic underachievement, substance abuse, and involvement in delinquent activities.

In adulthood, ADHD symptoms can affect various domains of functioning, including education, employment, and interpersonal relationships. Challenges in organization, time management, and emotional regulation may persist, necessitating adaptive strategies and accommodations to navigate the demands of adulthood successfully.

Despite the challenges posed by ADHD, many individuals with the disorder demonstrate **resilience, creativity, and strengths** in specific areas. With appropriate support, interventions, and self-management strategies, you can capitalize on your strengths, overcome obstacles, and achieve success in various aspects of your life.

Chapter 1

Why You Need to Manage ADHD

Effectively managing the symptoms of Attention Deficit Hyperactivity Disorder (ADHD) is crucial for enhancing daily functioning and improving quality of life.

Numerous studies have shown that unmanaged ADHD symptoms can significantly impact academic and occupational performance. Children with untreated ADHD often struggle in school, experiencing difficulties with attention, organization, and completing tasks. Academic underachievement, lower grades, and increased risk of academic failure are commonly observed outcomes among students with untreated ADHD. Unfortunately, many parents don't know these things so they think children (who are actually suffering from ADHD) are not serious or indolent. As a sufferer, I faced a lot of problems during this aspect of my life because my parents where never exposed to the symptoms of ADHD. If you're a parent, you've taken a significant step towards learning more about this developmental disability, which will greatly help you not only to understand your child with ADHD but also guide them properly.

However, if you're an adult with ADHD, you may encounter challenges in the workplace, including difficulties with time management, organization, and meeting deadlines. This time, you're not monitoring someone and helping them manage their symptoms. Rather, you're focusing on yourself and addressing the problem through proactive action.

When you don't address these symptoms, they can impede your career advancement, job satisfaction, and professional success. Research suggests that individuals with ADHD are at higher risk of unemployment, job instability, and occupational underachievement compared to their neurotypical counterparts.

Social Relationships

Managing ADHD symptoms is essential for fostering positive social relationships and interpersonal functioning. Children and adults with ADHD may struggle with impulsivity, social inhibition, and difficulties in understanding social cues, making it challenging to establish and maintain friendships and romantic relationships.

Untreated ADHD symptoms can contribute to social difficulties, such as frequent conflicts, social rejection, and feelings of isolation. Moreover, people with this condition are at increased risk of experiencing peer rejection, bullying, and social withdrawal, which can have adverse effects on self-esteem and mental well-being.

Addressing ADHD symptoms through interventions, such as behavioral therapy and medication management, can improve social skills, enhance self-awareness, and facilitate more positive social interactions.

Building effective communication strategies, practicing empathy, and developing healthy coping mechanisms are essential components of managing ADHD symptoms in social contexts.

We're going to be talking about these strategies in the later part of this book to help you upgrade your social relationships.

Emotional Well-being

Equally, untreated ADHD symptoms can have a profound impact on emotional well-being, leading to increased stress, anxiety, and mood disturbances. As an adult with ADHD, you might experience difficulties in regulating your emotions, coping with frustration, and managing stressors effectively.

Some studies suggest that people suffering from ADHD are at higher risk of developing **comorbid mental health conditions**, such as anxiety disorders, depression, and substance abuse. The presence of untreated ADHD symptoms can exacerbate emotional dysregulation, impair coping mechanisms, and contribute to a cycle of negative affectivity.

Managing ADHD symptoms through interventions, such as cognitive-behavioral therapy and mindfulness-based practices, can promote emotional resilience, enhance coping skills, and reduce the risk of developing comorbid mental health conditions.

Learning to identify and challenge negative thought patterns, practicing relaxation techniques, and seeking social support are essential strategies for promoting emotional well-being in individuals with ADHD. These techniques will also be discussed in the later part of this book to help you improve your emotional well-being.

Long-term Outcomes

The importance of managing ADHD symptoms extends beyond immediate daily functioning to long-term outcomes across the lifespan.

If you leave your ADHD symptoms untreated, there might be adverse long-term outcomes, including occupational instability and impaired social relationships.

However, early intervention and effective symptom management can mitigate these negative outcomes and promote positive developmental trajectories.

Children who receive timely diagnosis and appropriate interventions for ADHD are more likely to experience academic success, develop adaptive skills, and establish fulfilling social relationships.

In adulthood, managing ADHD symptoms can lead to improved occupational functioning, higher levels of job satisfaction, and enhanced well-being.

PURPOSE OF THIS BOOK

This book will serves as a comprehensive resource designed to empower you to effectively manage your symptoms and improve your daily functioning. The purpose is multifaceted, aiming to provide practical strategies, tips, and prompts tailored to address the diverse challenges associated with ADHD.

This solution deck takes a holistic approach to ADHD management, covering a wide range of topics relevant to daily functioning.

From organization and time management to attention regulation and emotional well-being, each section addresses key aspects of ADHD symptomatology, ensuring comprehensive support for individuals across different life domains.

Rather than simply providing theoretical concepts, the book offers practical strategies, tips, prompts, and life experiences that you can immediately implement in your daily life.

Whether it's creating a structured routine, using visual aids for organization, or practicing mindfulness exercises, the book provides actionable guidance aimed at improving functioning and reducing the impact of ADHD symptoms.

By equipping you with practical tools and resources, this book empowers you to take an active role in managing your ADHD symptoms and advocating for your needs. Through self-directed learning and skill-building, you can cultivate greater self-awareness, confidence, and resilience in navigating the challenges of ADHD.

Finally, this resource fosters a supportive and non-judgmental environment for anyone who want to manage ADHD, acknowledging the diverse experiences and struggles associated with the condition.

Chapter 2

Time Management Techniques

One of the fundamental aspects of effective management is setting realistic goals and priorities, especially for individuals with ADHD who may struggle with **impulsivity and distractibility**. Establishing clear goals and priorities can enhance your focus, motivation, and productivity. Here are actionable tips for setting realistic goals and priorities:

Identify Your Values

Begin by clarifying your values, aspirations, and long-term objectives. Consider what matters most to you personally and professionally, and identify overarching goals that align with your values.

Reflect on your priorities in various areas of life, such as career, relationships, health, and personal development.

Break Down Goals into Smaller Steps

Once you've identified your *overarching goals*, break them down into smaller, actionable steps or milestones. I've found that breaking down my goals into smaller, achievable chunks help me focus better and less overwhelmed.

Focus on completing one task or sub-task at a time, rather than trying to tackle everything at once. Breaking goals into manageable components makes them more attainable and provides a clear roadmap for progress. Focus on identifying specific actions you can take to move closer to your goals.

Most importantly, breaking tasks into smaller components reduces overwhelm and makes it easier to make progress consistently.

Set SMART Goals

Use the SMART criteria (Specific, Measurable, Achievable, Relevant, Time-bound) to structure your goals in a way that enhances clarity and accountability.

Ensure that each goal is specific, measurable, attainable, relevant to your objectives, and has a **defined timeline for completion**. SMART goals provide a framework for setting realistic and actionable objectives.

I've found Parkinson's Law to be relevant here and have found it extremely useful in getting things done. Whenever

I put time on a task, I've usually pushed to do it or I start developing FOMO (fear of missing out). I'm also more likely to do it with full attention when I have to work with a time constrain.

Be Realistic

Realize that you won't always concentrate. You'll sometimes fail to achieve your goals. And you'll find it hard to say on track at some point. What you don't want is unrealistic expectations about what you can achieve or do at any particular time.

What you should rather do is set realistic expectations for what you can accomplish within a given timeframe, taking into account your capabilities, resources, and external constraints.

Avoid overcommitting or setting overly ambitious goals that may lead to frustration or burnout. Be honest with yourself about what you can realistically achieve, and focus on making incremental progress over time.

Consider Potential Challenges

Anticipate potential challenges that may arise as you work towards your goals, and develop strategies to address them proactively.

Identify potential barriers, such as time constraints, distractions, or competing priorities, and brainstorm solutions to overcome them. Having contingency plans in place helps you navigate setbacks and stay on track with your goals.

What I try to do is to factor possible obstacles I may face while trying to achieve my goals during the planning stage. This way, I'm not take unaware if I suddenly have to face a challenge to reach a milestone.

Monitor Progress

I can't emphasize this enough. It can mean the difference between being productive and wasting time. When I look at my goals, I don't just want to see that I'm achieving them but also want to see improvements.

I want to be able to say I've improved a lot this year in various aspects of my life when compared to the previous year.

So, I'll recommend you regularly monitor your progress towards your goals and adjust your approach as needed based on feedback and results.

Track your achievements, celebrate successes, and identify areas for improvement or refinement. Be flexible and adaptive, willing to adjust your goals or strategies as circumstances change or new information emerges.

Review and Reassess

Set aside time regularly to review your goals, priorities, and progress. Reflect on what's working well and what could be improved, and make adjustments as needed to stay aligned with your objectives.

Regular review and reassessment ensure that your goals remain relevant and achievable in light of changing circumstances.

USING TIMERS OR ALARMS TO STAY ON TRACK

Using timers or alarms is a practical and effective strategy for managing time, staying focused, and maintaining high levels of productivity. Timers and alarms can help you overcome procrastination, reduce distractions, and improve your productivity. To benefit most from these tools, you need to do some of the following:

Set Clear Objectives

Before using timers or alarms, establish clear objectives for the tasks or activities you want to accomplish.

Define what you aim to achieve within a specific time frame, whether it's completing a task, staying focused on a project, or taking a break.

Having clear objectives ensures that you use timers or alarms purposefully to support your goals.

Choose the Right Tool

Select a timer or alarm tool that suits your preferences and needs. You can use a variety of tools, including digital timers, smartphone apps, kitchen timers, or wearable devices.

Choose a tool that offers features such as customizable settings, multiple alarms, and easy accessibility to ensure it meets your requirements for time management.

Set Time Limits for Tasks

When starting a task or activity, set a specific time limit or duration for completing it. Use your timer or alarm to designate the allotted time, and commit to staying focused and productive until the timer goes off. Setting time limits helps create a sense of urgency and prevents tasks from dragging on indefinitely.

Use the Pomodoro Technique

Consider implementing the Pomodoro Technique, a popular time management method that involves working in short, focused bursts followed by brief breaks. Set your timer for a predetermined work interval (usually 25 minutes), known as a "Pomodoro," followed by a short break (typically 5 minutes). After completing four Pomodoros, take a longer break (15-30 minutes) before resuming work.

I've tried the Pomodoro Technique a couple of time but it didn't work for me. And that's because I am easily overwhelmed and can't shake off the *"feelings of being restraint"*. However, I've found a workaround.

Instead of using an alarm or setting a time for a task, I setup a mental picture of how long I want spend on the task. This way, I may spend 15, 25, or 30 minutes on the task, and move on to something else, without the feeling that I'm being *constrained*.

If it didn't work for me, why did I include it here? I've found a lot of people who stood by and believe in the power of the technique. It worked for them and they have incorporated it into their daily routine. Even though it technically didn't work for me, it may be an excellent productivity boost for you.

Set Reminders for Transitions

Use timers or alarms to signal transitions between different activities or tasks throughout your day. Set reminders to prompt you to switch tasks, take breaks, or move on to the next item on your agenda.

Transition reminders help maintain momentum, prevent procrastination, and keep you on track with your schedule.

I use this regularly and have found it to be extremely useful and productivity boosting. Because I forget things so easily, I sometimes need something to remind me what I should be doing at a particular time.

Setting reminders has filled that gap perfectly.

Experiment with Interval Timing

Another thing you can do is to experiment with interval timing to optimize your productivity and focus.

Some individuals find that alternating between periods of focused work and short breaks in specific intervals (e.g., 50 minutes of work followed by a 10-minute break) enhances their productivity and concentration.

Adjust your timer settings to find the interval timing that works best for you.

Incorporate Accountability

Use timers or alarms as a tool for accountability by sharing your goals and progress with a friend, colleague, or accountability partner.

Set timers together and commit to working on tasks simultaneously, checking in periodically to share updates and support each other's progress. Accountability can increase motivation and adherence to time management goals.

To be clear, I love working alone. A lot… But sometimes, it But when I consistently fail to stick to my agenda, I seek accountability from a close pal. While I don't do it regularly, it can be very handy as at when needed.

Adjust as Needed

Be flexible and willing to adjust your timer or alarm settings based on your evolving needs and preferences. If you find that a particular time limit or interval isn't effective, experiment with different settings until you find what works best for you. Regularly evaluate and refine your approach to maximize the benefits of using timers or alarms.

Celebrate Successes

Acknowledge and celebrate your accomplishments and milestones as you use timers or alarms to stay on track with your goals. Recognize the progress you've made, no matter how small, and reward yourself for staying focused and productive. Celebrating successes reinforces positive behavior and motivates continued use of timers or alarms for time management.

By incorporating timers or alarms into your time management strategy and following these actionable steps, individuals with ADHD can enhance their focus, productivity, and productivity. Timers and alarms provide structure, accountability, and external cues to help individuals stay on track with their goals and make the most of their time.

PRIORITIZING TASKS BASED ON URGENCY OF IMPORTANCE

Prioritizing tasks based on urgency and importance is a key aspect of effective time management, especially for someone with ADHD who may struggle with impulsivity and difficulty focusing.

This can also enhance productivity, reduce stress, and improve overall task completion skills.

Start by assessing the urgency of each task on your to-do list.

Determine which tasks require immediate attention and which ones can be deferred or postponed.

Urgency refers to how quickly a task needs to be completed to avoid negative consequences or missed deadlines.

Next, consider the importance or significance of each task in relation to your goals and objectives.

Ask yourself how each task contributes to your long-term priorities, values, or responsibilities.

Importance refers to the impact or relevance of a task to your broader goals.

Use the Eisenhower Matrix

Eisenhower Matrix, a time management tool, is used to categorize tasks based on their urgency and importance.

Here is how to use this technique:

1. Divide your tasks into four quadrants:

Quadrant 1: Urgent and Important (Do First) - Tasks that require immediate attention and are crucial to your goals.

Quadrant 2: Important but Not Urgent (Schedule) - Tasks that contribute to your long-term goals and priorities but don't require immediate action.

Quadrant 3: Urgent but Not Important (Delegate) - Tasks that are time-sensitive but don't align with your priorities. Consider delegating these tasks to others if possible.

Quadrant 4: Not Urgent and Not Important (Eliminate) - Tasks that are neither urgent nor important. Consider eliminating or minimizing these tasks to focus on more meaningful activities.

2. Prioritize Quadrant 1 Tasks:

Start by prioritizing tasks in Quadrant 1 (Urgent and Important). These tasks require immediate attention and should be addressed first to prevent negative consequences or missed deadlines. Focus on completing these tasks before moving on to less urgent or important tasks.

Schedule Quadrant 2 Tasks:

Next, schedule tasks in Quadrant 2 (Important but Not Urgent) for future completion. Allocate dedicated time slots in your schedule to work on these tasks, ensuring that they receive appropriate attention and effort. By proactively addressing important tasks, you can prevent them from becoming urgent in the future.

Delegate Quadrant 3 Tasks:

Evaluate tasks in Quadrant 3 (Urgent but Not Important) and consider whether they can be delegated to others. Delegate tasks that don't align with your priorities or expertise to appropriate individuals who can handle them more efficiently. Delegating tasks frees up your time and energy to focus on tasks that are more important and relevant to your goals.

Minimize Quadrant 4 Tasks:

Minimize or eliminate tasks in Quadrant 4 (Not Urgent and Not Important) to reduce distractions and focus on meaningful activities. Evaluate whether these tasks add value to your goals, and consider whether they can be delegated, automated, or eliminated altogether.

Use Time Blocking:

Implement time blocking techniques to allocate specific time slots for different types of tasks based on their urgency and importance. Dedicate blocks of time in your schedule for tackling Quadrant 1 tasks, scheduling Quadrant 2 tasks, and addressing other priorities as needed. Time blocking helps structure your day and ensures that you allocate sufficient time and attention to each task category.

Regularly reassess your task list and priorities to ensure that they remain aligned with your goals and objectives. Be flexible and willing to adjust your priorities as circumstances change or new information emerges. Reevaluate the urgency and importance of tasks and make adjustments to your schedule accordingly.

INCORPORATING BREAKS TO PREVENT OVERWHELM AND BURNOUT

Incorporating breaks is essential for preventing overwhelm, maintaining focus, and mitigating the risk of burnout. Research suggests that taking regular breaks throughout the day can improve cognitive function, enhance productivity, and reduce stress levels.

Remember I told you that I don't like using time-based techniques like the "Pomodoro Technique" to improve time management because it more than often leaves me overwhelmed. Here, I'll teach you how to incorporate breaks to prevent this kind of burnout.

But first, why breaks?

Breaks provide opportunities to rest, recharge, and replenish cognitive resources, allowing individuals to sustain focus and performance over time. Research indicates that taking regular breaks can improve concentration, creativity, and productivity.

Now, the first and most important:

Listen to Your Body and Mind

Pay attention to your body and mind's signals to identify when you need a break. Notice signs of fatigue, decreased concentration, or increased stress levels as indicators that it's time to take a break. Avoid pushing yourself to the point of exhaustion or burnout and prioritize self-care by incorporating breaks into your daily routine.

Schedule Regular Breaks

Most of the times, it is your body that will tell you when to rest. However, you may sometimes need to be proactive, rather than just depending on your body to tell you when to rest.

Intentionally schedule breaks throughout your day to ensure that you prioritize rest and relaxation. Set aside dedicated time slots for breaks in your schedule, incorporating both short breaks (e.g., 5-10 minutes) and longer breaks (e.g., 15-30 minutes) as needed. Consider timing your breaks strategically, such as mid-morning and mid-afternoon, to coincide with natural energy fluctuations.

Use Physical Activity

Use breaks as opportunities to incorporate movement and physical activity into your routine. Engage in light stretching, walking, or other low-impact exercises to promote circulation, reduce muscle tension, and boost energy levels. Physical activity during breaks can enhance mood, cognitive function, and well-being.

Disconnect and Unplug

During breaks, disconnect from electronic devices and unplug from digital distractions to give your brain a break from constant stimulation. Step away from screens, emails, and social media to allow your mind to rest and recharge. Use break time to engage in activities that promote relaxation and mindfulness, such as reading, meditating, or enjoying nature.

Engage in Enjoyable Activities

Use breaks as opportunities to engage in activities that you find enjoyable and rejuvenating. Pursue hobbies, interests, or leisure activities that bring you joy and relaxation. Whether it's listening to an audio book, spending time outdoors, or practicing a creative pursuit, prioritize activities that help you unwind and recharge during breaks.

Practice Mindfulness

Incorporate mindfulness techniques and deep breathing exercises into your break routine to promote relaxation and stress reduction. Take a few minutes to focus on your breath, practicing deep, diaphragmatic breathing to calm the nervous system and induce a state of relaxation.

Mindfulness practices during breaks can improve focus, clarity, and emotional well-being. I have found mindfulness techniques and deep breathing exercises to be extremely soothing, especially when I'm highly tensed. Right now, I'm still working on how to fully incorporate it into my daily activities.

Set Boundaries. Honor Your Breaks

Establish boundaries to protect your break time and ensure that you prioritize self-care. Communicate your break schedule to colleagues, family members, or roommates, and encourage them to respect your designated break times. Honor your breaks as non-negotiable opportunities for self-renewal and rejuvenation.

Monitor Break Effectiveness

Reflect on the impact of breaks on your welfare and productivity. Notice how taking regular breaks influences your energy levels, focus, and mood throughout the day. Adjust your break routine as needed based on feedback from your body and mind to optimize their effectiveness.

Cultivate a Break-Friendly Culture

Promote a break-friendly culture in your workplace or environment by encouraging colleagues or peers to prioritize rest and relaxation. Lead by example by taking regular breaks and advocating for breaks as essential components of a healthy and productive work environment.

Foster a culture that values well-being and recognizes the importance of incorporating breaks into daily routines.

Chapter 3

Organization Strategies

In order to become a highly organized person, regardless of your ADHD symptoms, there are many strategies you can utilize. But some of the most important, that'll give the most impact, is learning how to use calendars and planners effectively, develop powerful routines, and know how to maximize any available space you have – whether at home or at work. We'll start with how to use calendars and planners effectively.

LEARN TO USE CALENDARS AND PLANNERS EFFECTIVELY

Effective utilization of calendars and planners is a cornerstone of organization for individuals with ADHD, offering a structured approach to managing time, tasks, and responsibilities. Research and anecdotal evidence highlight the efficacy of this strategy in improving time management, reducing forgetfulness, and enhancing overall productivity.

Here's why utilizing calendars and planners effectively is essential:

Time Management:

Calendars and planners provide a visual representation of time, allowing individuals to schedule activities, appointments, and deadlines systematically. Research indicates that those suffering from ADHD often struggle with time perception and time estimation, leading to difficulties in prioritizing tasks and allocating time effectively. By using calendars and planners to schedule activities and allocate specific time slots for tasks, you can improve your time management skills and reduce procrastination.

Organization:

One of the core challenges associated with ADHD is difficulties in organization and task management. Calendars and planners serve as organizational tools, helping individuals keep track of important dates, events, and commitments. When you record tasks and deadlines in a centralized location, you'll be able to avoid missed appointments, deadlines, and obligations, leading to greater efficiency and productivity.

Visual Cues and Reminders:

The visual nature of calendars and planners provides tangible cues and reminders to help you stay on track with your schedules and tasks.

Color-coding, highlighting, and using visual symbols can enhance the visibility of important events and deadlines, making it easier for you to prioritize tasks and manage your time effectively.

Additionally, setting alerts and reminders on digital calendars or mobile devices can provide auditory cues to prompt task initiation and completion.

Reduced Cognitive Load:

Individuals with ADHD often experience cognitive overload, making it challenging to keep track of multiple tasks and responsibilities simultaneously. Calendars and planners serve as external aids, offloading cognitive demands by providing a structured framework for organizing information and planning activities.

By externalizing tasks and deadlines, individuals can alleviate mental strain and improve cognitive functioning, leading to enhanced focus and productivity.

Flexibility and Adaptability:

Calendars and planners offer flexibility and adaptability to accommodate changing schedules and priorities. Individuals may encounter unexpected events, interruptions, or delays that disrupt their plans. Calendars and planners allow for adjustments and revisions to schedules, enabling individuals to adapt to unforeseen circumstances while maintaining a sense of control and organization.

Sense of Accomplishment:

Regularly using calendars and planners can foster a sense of accomplishment and satisfaction as you track your progress and check off completed tasks. Experiencing this sense of *mastery* and *achievement* is essential for promoting motivation and self-esteem. By visually documenting your accomplishments and successes, not only can you reinforce positive behaviors and habits, but can further enhance your organizational skills and self-efficacy.

ACTIONABLE TIPS FOR EFFECTIVELY USING CALENDARS & PLANNERS

Select a calendar or planner format that aligns with your preferences and needs.

Whether you prefer a paper-based planner, digital calendar, or a combination of both, choose a format that you feel comfortable using consistently. Consider factors such as portability, ease of use, and compatibility with your lifestyle and routine.

Designate a centralized location for recording tasks, appointments, and deadlines.

Whether it's a physical planner, a digital calendar app, or a combination of both, having a single, accessible location ensures that you can easily reference and update your schedule as needed. Avoid scattering information across multiple platforms to minimize confusion and streamline organization.

Set aside dedicated time each day or week to review and update your calendar or planner.

Use this time to add new tasks, revise existing plans, and prioritize upcoming commitments.

Regular check-ins help you stay organized, anticipate upcoming events, and adjust your schedule as needed to accommodate changing priorities.

Establish a consistent formatting system for recording information in your calendar or planner. Use color-coding, symbols, or categories to differentiate between different types of activities, such as work tasks, personal appointments, and social events.

Consistent formatting enhances visibility and clarity, making it easier to interpret and navigate your schedule at a glance.

When scheduling tasks and appointments, be mindful of your time constraints and limitations.

Avoid overcommitting by accurately estimating the time required to complete each task. Factor in buffer time for unforeseen delays or interruptions to prevent schedule overrun and reduce stress.

Take advantage of reminders and alerts to keep you on track with your schedule.

Set notifications for upcoming appointments, deadlines, and important tasks to ensure that you don't miss anything.

Use a combination of visual, auditory, and mobile alerts to accommodate different preferences and ensure timely reminders.

CREATE DESIGNATED SPACES FOR IMPORTANT ITEMS

Creating designated spaces for important items is a practical strategy to improve organization and reduce the risk of misplacing or losing belongings, which can be extremely useful for those of us who may struggle with forgetfulness and disorganization.

Establishing designated spaces can also enhance retrieval efficiency and promote organization habits. Here are some of the things you can do to maximize space in your home or office:

Identify Frequently Used Items:

Start by identifying the items that you use regularly and consider essential for your daily activities.

These may include keys, wallets, phones, chargers, medication, important documents, and other commonly used belongings.

Take inventory of the items you frequently use to determine which ones require designated spaces.

Assess Usage Patterns and Accessibility:

Consider how often you use each item and where you typically need access to them. Items that are used daily or multiple times throughout the day should be stored in easily accessible locations.

Assess your daily routines and habits to determine the most convenient placement for each item based on usage patterns.

Designate Specific Locations:

Assign a specific location or storage area for each item based on its frequency of use and relevance to your daily activities.

Choose locations that are easily accessible, visible, and consistent to facilitate retrieval and minimize the likelihood of misplacement. Use labels, containers, or organizers to clearly delineate designated spaces for each item.

Establish a Home for Each Item:

Designate a "home" or dedicated spot for each item where it will reside when not in use.

Consistency is key to maintaining organization, so be diligent about returning items to their designated homes after use. Encourage household members to respect and adhere to the designated storage locations to maintain order and minimize confusion.

Customize Organization Systems:

Tailor organization systems to suit your individual preferences, habits, and living space. Consider factors such as available storage space, aesthetic preferences, and lifestyle needs when designing organization solutions.

Experiment with different storage solutions, such as hooks, shelves, baskets, or drawer organizers, to find what works best for you.

Implement Visual Cues:

Use visual cues and reminders to reinforce designated storage locations and encourage adherence to organization systems.

Label storage containers, shelves, or drawers with descriptive labels or visual symbols to indicate the contents and purpose of each storage area.

Visual cues help prompt memory retrieval and facilitate consistent organization habits.

Practice Consistent Maintenance:

Establish a routine for maintaining organization and tidiness in designated storage areas. Schedule regular maintenance sessions to declutter, reorganize, and reassess storage solutions as needed. Consistent upkeep is essential for preventing clutter buildup and ensuring that designated spaces remain functional and accessible.

Involve Household Members:

If applicable, involve household members in the organization process and encourage their participation in maintaining designated spaces. Most will be happy to participate, especially if it is something that affects everyone in the home.

Collaborate with family members or roommates to establish shared organization systems and ensure everyone understands and respects designated storage locations. Foster a collaborative approach to organization to promote accountability and cohesion within the household.

TAKE ADVANTAGE OF ESTABLISHED ROUTINES AND SCHEDULES

As I hinted above, implementing routines and schedules is a highly effective strategy for you to establish structure, manage time, and improve daily functioning. Some studies have even suggests that adherence to routines and schedules can enhance productivity, reduce procrastination, and alleviate feelings of overwhelm.

Establish Consistent Wake-Up and Bedtime Routines:

Start your day off right by establishing consistent wake-up and bedtime routines. Set a regular wake-up time and bedtime to regulate your sleep-wake cycle and promote healthy sleep habits.

Incorporate calming activities into your bedtime routine to signal to your body that it's time to wind down and prepare for sleep.

Plan and Prioritize Daily Activities:

Use a planner or calendar to schedule and prioritize your daily activities and tasks. Allocate specific time blocks for each task, appointment, or obligation, and prioritize them based on urgency and importance.

Break down larger tasks into smaller, manageable steps and schedule them throughout the day to facilitate progress and prevent overwhelm.

Allocate Time for Routine Tasks:

Identify routine tasks and responsibilities that require regular attention, such as household chores, meal preparation, exercise, and self-care activities.

Allocate dedicated time slots for these tasks in your daily schedule to ensure they are consistently addressed. Incorporating routine tasks into your schedule helps establish predictability and consistency in your daily routine.

Create Morning and Evening Rituals:

Establish morning and evening rituals to bookend your day with structure and intention. Designate specific activities to include in your morning and evening routines, such as journaling, exercise, meditation, or reflection.

Morning rituals can help you start your day on a positive note, while evening rituals can help you unwind and transition into relaxation mode.

Set Time Limits and Boundaries:

Be mindful of time limits and boundaries when scheduling activities and tasks. Avoid overcommitting or overscheduling yourself, as this can lead to feelings of stress and overwhelm. Set realistic expectations for what you can accomplish within a given time frame and be prepared to adjust your schedule as needed to maintain balance and prevent burnout.

Stick to a Regular Routine:

Consistency is key to successful implementation of routines and schedules. Strive to stick to your established routines and schedules as closely as possible, even on weekends or during periods of disruption. Consistent adherence to routines promotes predictability, reduces decision fatigue, and enhances productivity and well-being.

Chapter 4

Attention Regulation Tips

Regularly maintaining your attention is something that's extremely difficult. In fact, I'm still battling with it. However, after doing some of these things, I've seen a lot of improvement.

Fortunately, the more improvement you see, the more your motivation builds up.

Here, I'll be detailing some of the things that worked for me and others and can work for you too. They are anecdotal and not necessarily backed by science. But if it works for you, why worry?

So, if you want to ensure you're regularly maintaining your focus on tasks, these are some of the things you can do to enhance your attention regulation skills:

1. Identify Common Distractions

Start by identifying common sources of distraction in your environment. These may include noisy environments, cluttered workspaces, digital devices, social media notifications, or interruptions from colleagues or family members. Awareness of potential distractions is the first step toward effectively managing them.

2. Create a Distraction-Free Workspace

Designate a specific area or workspace that is free from distractions and conducive to focus. Choose a quiet, well-lit space with minimal visual and auditory distractions. Keep your workspace organized and clutter-free to reduce visual stimuli and promote a sense of calm and order.

3. Use Noise-Canceling Headphones

Invest in noise-canceling headphones to block out background noise and create a more tranquil work environment. Noise-canceling technology can help drown out distracting sounds, such as conversations, traffic noise, or household activities, allowing you to concentrate more effectively on tasks.

4. Set Boundaries with Others

Communicate your need for focus and concentration to colleagues, family members, or roommates, and establish clear boundaries around your work time. Encourage others to respect your designated work hours and minimize interruptions or distractions during those times. Establishing boundaries helps create a conducive environment for sustained attention.

5. Limit Digital Distractions

Minimize digital distractions by implementing strategies to manage your use of electronic devices. Turn off non-essential notifications on your smartphone, computer, or tablet to reduce interruptions from incoming emails, messages, or social media alerts. Use apps or browser extensions that block distracting websites or limit screen time during focused work sessions.

6. Schedule Dedicated Focus Time

Allocate dedicated blocks of time for focused work or deep concentration without distractions. Schedule specific time slots in your calendar for uninterrupted work sessions, and commit to staying off digital devices and avoiding multitasking during these periods. Setting aside focused work time enhances productivity and minimizes distractions.

7. Optimize Lighting Conditions

Ensure that your workspace is well-lit with natural or artificial lighting that is comfortable for sustained focus. Adjust lighting conditions to minimize glare, shadows, or harsh lighting that may cause eye strain or fatigue.

Optimizing lighting enhances visual comfort and promotes alertness during tasks.

8. Experiment with Environmental Modifications

Experiment with environmental modifications to optimize your workspace for focus and productivity. Consider factors such as temperature, air quality, and ergonomic comfort to create an environment that supports sustained attention. Personalize your workspace to suit your preferences and sensory needs, making adjustments as needed to minimize distractions.

USING THE "CHUNKING TECHNIQUE"

We have discussed this briefly under time management, but will go deeper here. This is because implementing the "chunking" technique can be a valuable strategy to improve focus and productivity by breaking tasks into smaller, more manageable chunks.

Research suggests that chunking tasks into smaller components can enhance cognitive processing, reduce feelings of overwhelm, and promote improved productivity. Here are actionable steps for implementing the chunking technique:

Break Tasks into Smaller Steps:

Start by breaking down larger tasks or projects into smaller, actionable steps or subtasks. Identify the individual components or actions required to complete the task effectively. Breaking tasks into smaller steps makes them more manageable and reduces the cognitive load associated with complex tasks.

Define Clear Milestones:

Establish clear milestones or checkpoints to mark progress as you work through each step of the task. Set specific criteria or objectives for reaching each milestone, providing clarity and direction for your efforts. Clear milestones help track progress and maintain momentum towards completing the task.

Prioritize Subtasks:

Prioritize subtasks based on their importance and urgency relative to the task. Identify which subtasks are essential for moving the project forward and which ones can be addressed later. Focus on tackling high-priority subtasks first to ensure that you make meaningful progress towards task completion.

Allocate Time for Each Chunk:

Allocate dedicated time blocks for working on each chunk or subtask of the larger task. Set realistic time limits for completing each component, taking into account factors such as complexity, difficulty, and available resources. Time boxing ensures that you allocate sufficient time and attention to each chunk while preventing procrastination or perfectionism.

Focus on One Chunk at a Time:

Concentrate your attention on one chunk or subtask at a time, avoiding multitasking or attempting to address multiple components simultaneously. By focusing on one chunk at a time, you can maintain clarity, reduce distractions, and optimize cognitive resources for effective task completion.

Use Visual Aids or Organizers:

Utilize visual aids or organizers, such as lists, charts, or mind maps, to visually represent the breakdown of tasks into smaller chunks. Visual tools help clarify the relationship between different components of the task and provide a tangible reference for tracking progress. Use color coding or highlighting to distinguish between different subtasks.

PRACTICING MINDFULNESS AND MEDITATION

Practicing mindfulness and using meditation exercises is another beneficial method for enhancing focus, reducing distractibility, and promoting attention regulation. It can improve cognitive function, emotional regulation, and good health. Fortunately, it's an easy thing to do. I try to do it regularly and have found it to be useful in stabilizing my attention.

I usually start with mindful breathing, so I'll recommend you begin with that too. Before you do that, you need to first set aside time and space for the activities.

Set Aside Dedicated Practice Time

Allocate dedicated time each day for practicing mindfulness and meditation exercises. Schedule sessions in your calendar and treat them as non-negotiable appointments with yourself.

Start with short practice sessions (e.g., 5-10 minutes) and gradually increase the duration as you build consistency and confidence in your practice. Regularity is key to reaping the benefits of mindfulness.

Create a Quiet, Calm Environment

Create a quiet, calm environment conducive to mindfulness practice by minimizing distractions and external stimuli. Find a comfortable space free from noise, interruptions, and visual clutter where you can focus without disturbance. Dim the lights, close curtains or blinds, and create a sense of tranquility to support deepening into your practice.

Mindful Breathing

Begin by practicing mindful breathing exercises to anchor your attention and cultivate present-moment awareness.

Find a comfortable seated position and focus your attention on the sensation of your breath as it enters and leaves your body.

Notice the rise and fall of your chest or the sensation of air passing through your nostrils.

Use your breath as a focal point to anchor your attention and bring your mind into the present moment.

Body Scan Meditation

Body scan meditation promotes bodily awareness and helps quiet the mind.

Engage in body scan meditation to increase awareness of physical sensations and promote relaxation.

Close your eyes and systematically scan your body from head to toe, paying attention to any areas of tension, discomfort, or relaxation.

Notice sensations without judgment, allowing tension to release and muscles to relax as you bring awareness to each part of your body.

Guided Meditation

Explore guided meditation practices designed to enhance focus and attention. It also provides support and guidance for those new to mindfulness.

Listen to guided meditation recordings or apps that offer structured exercises for cultivating mindfulness and concentration.

Follow along with the guidance provided, focusing on instructions for breath awareness, body relaxation, or visualization techniques.

Mindful Movement

Integrate mindful movement practices, such as yoga or Tai Chi, into your routine to promote body-mind connection and improve focus.

Engage in gentle, flowing movements coordinated with breath awareness to cultivate mindfulness and relaxation. Mindful movement practices encourage present-moment awareness, balance, and mental clarity, making them valuable complements to seated meditation.

Cultivate Non-Judgmental Awareness

Practice cultivating non-judgmental awareness of your thoughts, emotions, and sensory experiences during meditation. Notice thoughts as they arise without getting caught up in them or judging them as good or bad.

Embrace a stance of curiosity and acceptance towards whatever arises in your awareness, allowing experiences to come and go without attachment.

Be Patient and Gentle with Yourself

Approach mindfulness practice with patience, kindness, and self-compassion, recognizing that it's normal to experience fluctuations in attention and concentration.

Be gentle with yourself if your mind wanders or if you encounter challenges during meditation. Cultivate an attitude of openness and curiosity towards your experiences, embracing them as opportunities for growth and learning.

Apply Mindfulness to Daily Activities

Extend mindfulness beyond formal meditation practice by incorporating it into daily activities and routines. Practice mindful eating by savoring each bite of food and paying attention to flavors, textures, and sensations.

Bring mindfulness to routine tasks such as washing dishes, walking, or commuting by bringing full awareness to the present moment experience.

USING FIDGET TOOLS TO MAINTAIN FOCUS

Start by identifying suitable fidget tools or objects that provide tactile stimulation and promote movement without causing distraction to others. Explore a variety of options, such as stress balls, fidget spinners, textured toys, or hand-held gadgets, to find what works best for you. Choose fidget tools that are discreet, portable, and satisfying to manipulate.

Keep Fidget Tools Accessible:

Ensure that fidget tools are readily accessible and available whenever you need them to maintain focus. Keep fidget tools within arm's reach at your workspace, in your pocket, or in a designated fidget kit or container.

Having easy access to fidget tools allows you to use them as needed to manage restlessness or fidgeting behaviors.

Be Strategic:

Use fidget tools strategically during tasks that require sustained attention or concentration.

Engage in tactile stimulation with fidget tools while listening to lectures, participating in meetings, or working on assignments to help channel excess energy and maintain focus. Experiment with different fidget tools to determine which ones enhance your productivity without causing distraction.

Rotate Fidget Tools:

Rotate between different fidget tools or tactile objects to prevent habituation and maintain novelty. Experiment with various textures, shapes, and sensations to keep fidgeting engaging and enjoyable. Rotate fidget tools regularly to prevent boredom and maximize their effectiveness for maintaining focus and attention.

Chapter 5

Problem-Solving Prompts

IDENTIFYING COMMON CHALLENGES RELATED TO ADHD SYMPTOMS

This is an essential step if you want to better understand your experiences and develop effective strategies for managing symptoms. By recognizing common challenges, you can address them proactively and seek appropriate support. Here are key insights and information to help you identify common challenges related to ADHD symptoms:

1. Executive Functioning Difficulties

As someone suffering from ADHD, you may often experience challenges related to executive functioning, which encompasses cognitive processes such as planning, organization, time management, and impulse control.

Executive function deficits can manifest as difficulty in prioritizing tasks, maintaining focus, managing time effectively, and regulating emotions. To address these difficulties, effective solutions may include:

- **Use of External Tools:** Use of external tools such as planners, calendars, task lists, or mobile apps to help with organization and time management. These tools provide visual cues and reminders to aid in planning and prioritizing tasks effectively.
- **Break Tasks into Smaller Steps:** Try and break down tasks into smaller, manageable steps to reduce overwhelm and facilitate progress. By dividing larger tasks into smaller, actionable steps, you can approach them more systematically and feel a sense of accomplishment as you complete each step.
- **Implement Routine and Structure:** Establishing consistent routines and structures can help you better manage your time and activities. Engage in the creation of daily schedules that include designated times for specific tasks, activities, and breaks to promote organization and productivity.
- **Develop Self-Monitoring Skills:** Learn to monitor your own behavior and progress towards goals by setting up systems for self-assessment and reflection. Use self-monitoring tools such as checklists, self-rating scales, or journaling to track tasks, achievements, and areas for improvement.

2. Impulsivity and Hyperactivity

Impulsivity and hyperactivity are hallmark symptoms of ADHD, often resulting in impulsive decision-making, restless behavior, and difficulty sitting still or staying focused for extended periods. Impulsivity can lead to issues such as interrupting others, speaking out of turn, acting on impulse without considering consequences, and engaging in risky behaviors. Here is how to resolve this problem.

- **Practice Mindfulness and Self-awareness:** Practice mindfulness techniques to increase self-awareness and regulate impulsive behaviors. Mindfulness exercises, such as deep breathing or body scanning, can help individuals pause and respond thoughtfully rather than react impulsively.
- **Utilize Behavioral Strategies:** Implement behavioral strategies such as the use of self-monitoring, self-reinforcement, or self-regulation techniques to manage impulsive behaviors. Always pause and reflect before acting impulsively, and reward yourself for demonstrating self-control.
- **Engage in Regular Physical Activity:** Regular physical activity can help you channel excess energy and reduce hyperactivity. Participate in activities such as sports, yoga, or dance to promote physical health and regulate arousal levels.
- **Structured Environments and Routines:** Create structured environments and routines that provide clear expectations and guidelines for behavior. Establish consistent schedules, rules, and routines at

home, school, or work to manage impulsivity and stay on track.

3. Organization and Clutter

Individuals with ADHD frequently struggle with organization and clutter management, leading to disorganized living spaces, cluttered work environments, and difficulty finding or remembering important items. Organizational challenges can impact various areas of life, including home, school, work, and personal relationships, making organization and decluttering important.

- **Decluttering and Simplifying Spaces:** Declutter your living and workspaces regularly to reduce visual and mental distractions. Simplifying environments can make it easier to find items and maintain organization.

- **Use of Organization Systems:** Implement organization systems such as labeled containers, shelves, or storage bins to help you categorize and store items efficiently. Have in place clear guidelines for organizing your belongings and designate specific areas for different types of items.

- **Daily Maintenance Habits:** Promote daily maintenance habits such as tidying up at the end of each day or setting aside time for weekly organization sessions. Establishing consistent routines for maintaining order can prevent clutter from accumulating and improve overall organization.

- **Digital Organization Tools:** Utilize digital organization tools such as smartphone apps, note-taking apps, or task management software to keep track of appointments, tasks, and deadlines. You can also digitize documents, notes, and important information to reduce physical clutter.

4. Emotional Dysregulation

Emotional dysregulation is another common symptom you're likely to face. It is characterized by intense and fluctuating emotions, mood swings, and difficulty regulating reactions to stressors or frustrations. Emotional dysregulation can manifest as impulsivity, irritability, anger outbursts, anxiety, or depression, impacting interpersonal relationships and overall well-being. Here are some tips to navigate emotional dysregulation:

- **Develop Emotional Awareness:** Develop awareness of your emotions and recognize early signs of emotional dysregulation. Practice techniques such as mindfulness meditation or journaling to increase emotional self-awareness.
- **Implement Coping Strategies:** Develop coping strategies to manage intense emotions and regulate mood effectively. Techniques such as deep breathing exercises, progressive muscle relaxation, or guided imagery can help you calm your emotions and regain control.

- **Seek Professional Support:** Seek professional support from therapists or counselors trained in cognitive-behavioral therapy (CBT) or dialectical behavior therapy (DBT). Therapy can provide you with tools and strategies to improve emotional regulation skills and cope with intense emotions effectively.

5. Forgetfulness and Memory Problems

Forgetfulness and memory problems are prevalent among individuals with ADHD, leading to difficulties in remembering appointments, deadlines, commitments, or important information. Forgetfulness can result in missed appointments, misplaced items, and challenges in academic or professional settings.

- **Use of Memory Aids:** Make use of memory aids such as sticky notes, reminders on smartphones or digital calendars, and voice memos to help remember important tasks, appointments, and deadlines.

- **Establish Routines and Habits:** Establishing consistent routines and habits can help you compensate for memory difficulties. Encourage the use of daily routines for tasks such as morning and bedtime rituals, meal preparation, and studying.

- **Improve Sleep Hygiene:** Adequate sleep is essential for memory consolidation and cognitive function. Try to prioritize good sleep hygiene practices, such as maintaining a regular sleep schedule, creating a comfortable sleep environment, and avoiding stimulants like caffeine before bedtime.

- **Practice Memory Techniques:** Take advantage of enhancement techniques such as visualization, association, repetition, and chunking to improve memory recall. Use mnemonic devices or acronyms to aid in remembering information where needed.

6. Inattention and Distractibility:

Inattention and distractibility are core symptoms of ADHD, affecting concentration, focus, and sustained attention on tasks or activities. You might struggle to stay focused on tasks, become easily distracted by external stimuli, and have difficulty filtering out irrelevant information or noise in your environment.

- **Create a Distraction-Free Environment:** Create a quiet, clutter-free workspace with minimal distractions to enhance focus and concentration. Use noise-canceling headphones, white noise machines, or soundproofing techniques to minimize auditory distractions.
- **Use Visual Cues and Reminders:** Use visual cues and reminders to help you stay on task and maintain focus. Use visual schedules, checklists, or color-coded organizers to outline tasks and deadlines clearly.

- **Practice Mindfulness and Attention-Building Exercises:** Incorporate mindfulness practices and attention-building exercises into daily routines to improve focus and concentration. Techniques such as focused breathing, guided imagery, or mindfulness meditation so you can train your attentional skills further.

BRAINSTORMING POTENTIAL SOLUTIONS FOR SPECIFIC SITUATIONS

Brainstorming potential solutions for specific situations is a valuable skill for anyone to develop, as it empowers them to problem-solve and address challenges effectively.

You can brainstorm by first identifying the specific situation or challenge that needs to be addressed. Define the problem in concrete terms and consider its underlying causes and contributing factors.

Next, you need to gather relevant information about the situation, including any obstacles, constraints, or resources that may impact potential solutions. Conduct research, seek input from others, and gather data to inform the brainstorming process.

Put your creative powers to work and encourage open-mindedness by generating a wide range of potential solutions to the problem. Use techniques such as mind mapping, free association, or lateral thinking to generate new ideas and perspectives.

Evaluate each potential solution based on its feasibility, effectiveness, and alignment with the desired outcome. Consider the pros and cons of each solution, as well as any potential risks or unintended consequences.

Prioritize the potential solutions based on their likelihood of success and their potential impact on addressing the problem. Identify the most promising solutions that are practical, achievable, and well-suited to the situation.

Take action to implement the chosen solutions, following the action plans developed during the brainstorming process. Monitor progress, adjust strategies as needed, and celebrate successes along the way.

Reflect on the outcomes of the implemented solutions, assessing their effectiveness in addressing the problem and achieving the desired results. Identify lessons learned and areas for improvement to inform future problem-solving efforts.

Chapter 6

Emotional Regulation Strategies

Recognizing triggers for emotional dysregulation is the first and a critical aspect of emotional regulation strategies, especially for those who may be experiencing heightened emotional reactivity.

Understanding triggers helps you identify situations, thoughts, or emotions that may lead to emotional dysregulation, allowing for proactive intervention and management. Here are key considerations for recognizing triggers:

Identify Common Triggers:

Start by identifying common triggers or situations that tend to provoke emotional dysregulation. Triggers may include stressors related to work, relationships, academic pressure, or environmental factors. Pay attention to recurring patterns or themes in situations that evoke strong emotional responses, such as criticism, rejection, or feeling overwhelmed.

Reflect on Past Experiences:

Reflect on past experiences of emotional dysregulation to identify triggers and underlying patterns. Consider specific instances when you've felt intense emotions such as anger, frustration, anxiety, or sadness. Explore the circumstances, thoughts, or events that preceded these emotional reactions to gain insight into potential triggers.

Notice Physical and Emotional Signs:

Learn to recognize physical and emotional signs that indicate the onset of emotional dysregulation. Notice changes in your body, such as increased heart rate, muscle tension, shallow breathing, or sensations of heat or discomfort. Pay attention to emotional cues, such as irritability, agitation, sadness, or impulsivity, as indicators of heightened emotional arousal.

Keep a Trigger Journal:

Keep a trigger journal or diary to track situations, events, or thoughts that trigger emotional dysregulation. Record details about each trigger, including the context, emotions experienced, physical sensations, and thoughts or beliefs associated with the trigger. Tracking triggers over time helps identify patterns and provides valuable insight into emotional reactions.

Consider Cognitive Triggers:

Recognize cognitive triggers, such as negative self-talk, perfectionism, or catastrophizing, that contribute to emotional dysregulation. Notice recurring thought patterns or cognitive distortions that intensify emotional reactions and fuel maladaptive behaviors. Challenge distorted thinking patterns and replace them with more balanced and realistic perspectives.

Pay Attention to Environmental Factors:

Be mindful of environmental factors that may contribute to emotional dysregulation, such as sensory overload, noise, clutter, or chaotic surroundings. Notice how environmental stimuli impact your mood, energy levels, and ability to regulate emotions. Create a calm, soothing environment that supports emotional well-being and minimizes triggers.

Seek Feedback from Others:

Seek feedback from trusted friends, family members, or mental health professionals to gain insight into your triggers and emotional reactions. Ask others to share observations or perspectives on situations where you've experienced emotional dysregulation. External feedback can provide valuable insights and help identify blind spots.

Use Behavioral Cues as Indicators:

Pay attention to behavioral cues, such as impulsive actions, avoidance behaviors, or substance use, as indicators of emotional dysregulation. Notice patterns of behavior that occur in response to triggers and serve as coping mechanisms or maladaptive responses. Recognizing behavioral cues can help intervene early and prevent escalation of emotional distress.

DEVELOPING COPING MECHANISM FOR STRESS AND FRUSTRATION

Practice progressive muscle relaxation (PMR) to release tension and promote physical and mental relaxation. Start by tensing and then gradually relaxing different muscle groups in your body, starting from your toes and working your way up to your head. PMR helps reduce muscle tension, alleviate stress, and improve overall relaxation.

Use journaling as a therapeutic tool to express and process emotions, thoughts, and experiences. Write freely about your feelings, challenges, and successes, without judgment or censorship. Journaling promotes self-reflection, insight, and emotional release, providing a healthy outlet for managing stress and frustration.

Engage in creative activities that provide an outlet for self-expression and emotional release. Explore artistic pursuits such as painting, drawing, writing, music, or crafting. Creative outlets offer a means of channeling emotions, reducing stress, and fostering a sense of accomplishment and fulfillment.

Prioritize self-care activities that nourish your physical, emotional, and mental health. Engage in activities such as getting adequate sleep, maintaining a balanced diet, practicing good hygiene, and setting aside time for relaxation and leisure. Self-care practices replenish your energy reserves and enhance resilience to stress.

Utilize cognitive behavioral techniques to challenge negative thinking patterns and manage distressing emotions. Identify and reframe cognitive distortions, such as catastrophizing, black-and-white thinking, or personalizing situations. Replace negative thoughts with more balanced and realistic perspectives to reduce stress and improve coping.

Engaging in Regular Exercise

Engaging in regular exercise or physical activity is a powerful strategy to improve well-being, manage symptoms, and enhance cognitive function.

Exercise has been shown to positively impact mood, attention, and impulse control, making it an effective complement to traditional treatments for ADHD.

Here are actionable steps and relevant information to help you incorporate regular exercise into your routine:

Start with Realistic Goals:

Begin by setting realistic goals for incorporating regular exercise into your routine. Start with manageable objectives, such as aiming for 30 minutes of moderate-intensity exercise most days of the week.

Gradually increase the duration and intensity of your workouts as your fitness level improves.

Choose Activities You Enjoy:

Select physical activities that you enjoy and find engaging to increase motivation and adherence. Explore a variety of activities, such as walking, jogging, cycling, swimming, or team sports, to find what suits your interests and preferences. Variety keeps exercise enjoyable and prevents boredom.

Make Exercise a Priority:

Prioritize exercise by scheduling it into your daily or weekly routine, just like any other important commitment. Block out dedicated time slots for physical activity on your calendar and treat them as non-negotiable appointments with yourself. Consistency is key to reaping the benefits of regular exercise.

Start Slowly and Build Momentum:

Start with low-intensity activities and gradually increase the intensity and duration of your workouts over time. Listen to your body and avoid pushing yourself too hard, especially if you're new to exercise or have been inactive for a while. Focus on building momentum and establishing a sustainable exercise habit.

Experiment with Different Activities:

Stay open to experimenting with different types of exercise and activities to find what resonates with you. Mix up your routine with a combination of cardiovascular, strength training, flexibility, and balance exercises to reap diverse benefits. Variety prevents boredom and allows you to discover new ways to move your body.

Chapter 7

Medication Management

Understanding the role of medication in ADHD treatment is crucial to make informed decisions about managing symptoms effectively.

If possible, schedule an appointment with a qualified healthcare professional, such as a psychiatrist or primary care physician, to discuss ADHD symptoms and treatment options.

A healthcare provider can assess your symptoms, medical history, and treatment preferences to develop a personalized treatment plan.

But don't rely on that alone. Educate yourself about the different types of medications commonly used to treat ADHD, including stimulant and non-stimulant medications. Understand how these medications work in the brain to regulate neurotransmitters such as dopamine and norepinephrine, which play a role in attention, focus, and impulse control.

An important part of your education will be gaining knowledge about the potential benefits and risks associated with ADHD medications.

While medications can help you to effectively manage symptoms and improve functioning, they may also carry risks of side effects or adverse reactions.

Discuss the benefits and risks of medication with your healthcare provider to make informed decisions about treatment.

You also have the option of exploring different treatment options for ADHD, including medication, behavioral therapy, and lifestyle interventions.

Understand that medication is just one component of a comprehensive treatment plan and may be used in conjunction with other interventions to address ADHD symptoms effectively.

Once you start your medication, ensure to monitor their effects closely and communicate any concerns or changes in symptoms to your healthcare provider. Be proactive in discussing medication adjustments or changes based on individual response and treatment goals.

Recognize that managing ADHD is often a long-term process that may require ongoing medication management.

Work with your healthcare provider to develop a long-term treatment plan that addresses changing needs and goals over time.

ADHERING TO MEDICATION SCHEDULES AND ROUTINES

Adhering to medication schedules and routines is essential for maximizing the effectiveness of ADHD treatment and managing symptoms consistently.

Use alarms, smartphone apps, or medication reminder devices to set daily reminders for taking medication. I do this because I discover I forget easily and sometimes goes days not remembering I am on medication. So, it's very important to pay attention to this.

Consistency in medication timing is crucial for maintaining stable blood levels of the medication throughout the day.

To make it even easier, you can try to integrate medication-taking into existing daily routines, such as brushing teeth in the morning or evening, to establish a consistent habit. Associating medication with routine activities can help reinforce adherence.

Invest in pill organizers or medication trays to organize medications for each day of the week. Preparing medications in advance can streamline the process and reduce the risk of missed doses.

Another important step to take is storing medications in a visible location, such as on a countertop or near a frequently used area, to serve as a visual cue for medication adherence. Avoid storing medications in out-of-sight locations where they may be forgotten.

You can also keep a medication log or journal to track medication use and adherence. Record the date, time, and dosage of each medication taken to monitor adherence patterns and identify any missed doses.

TRACKING MEDICATION EFFECTIVENESS AND SIDE EFFECTS

Monitoring and tracking medication effectiveness and side effects is essential for those with ADHD to ensure optimal treatment outcomes and minimize potential risks.

Regularly assess ADHD symptoms and functioning to gauge the effectiveness of medication. Keep a symptom journal or diary to track changes in attention, focus, impulsivity, and hyperactivity over time.

Observe and document any side effects or adverse reactions experienced while taking ADHD medication.

Common side effects may include insomnia, decreased appetite, irritability, or headaches.

Communicate openly and honestly with healthcare providers about medication effectiveness and side effects. Be proactive in reporting any concerns or changes in symptoms to facilitate adjustments to the treatment plan.

Schedule regular follow-up appointments with healthcare providers to review medication effectiveness and side effects. Discuss any adjustments or modifications to the medication regimen based on individual response and treatment goals.

Consider using standardized rating scales or assessment tools to measure ADHD symptoms and functioning objectively. These tools can provide valuable insights into treatment progress and guide treatment decisions.

Monitor changes in mood, behavior, or physical health that may be related to medication use. Be vigilant for signs of potential medication misuse, dependence, or tolerance, and seek professional guidance if needed.

Finally, educate yourself about the potential long-term effects of ADHD medication and stay informed about the latest research findings. Make informed decisions about medication use based on a thorough understanding of the risks and benefits.

What can you do about side effects?

You can schedule appointments with your healthcare provider to discuss medication concerns or adjustments. Be proactive in addressing any issues or questions related to medication management.

Prepare for appointments by compiling a list of medication concerns, questions, or observations to discuss with the healthcare provider. Bring along any relevant documentation, such as medication logs or symptom journals, to facilitate the discussion.

Express concerns or uncertainties about medication openly and honestly with the healthcare provider. Share specific symptoms, side effects, or changes in functioning experienced while taking medication to provide a comprehensive picture of the treatment effects.

Ask questions about medication options, dosages, side effects, and potential interactions to gain a better understanding of the treatment plan. Seek clarification on any information that is unclear or confusing to ensure informed decision-making.

Discuss any changes in symptoms, functioning, or treatment goals since starting or adjusting medication.

Provide feedback on medication effectiveness and side effects to guide treatment decisions and adjustments.

Chapter 8

Financial Management

Let's start with budgeting techniques for tracking your income and expenses since they help you financial stability and achieving financial goals.

Begin by identifying and tracking all sources of income, including wages, salaries, bonuses, freelance earnings, or investment income. Having a clear understanding of your total income is essential for creating an accurate budget.

Make a comprehensive list of all monthly expenses, including fixed expenses (such as rent or mortgage, utilities, insurance premiums) and variable expenses (such as groceries, dining out, and entertainment).

Differentiate between essential needs and discretionary wants when categorizing expenses. Prioritize essential expenses that are necessary for daily living, such as housing, food, and transportation.

Set aside a portion of your income for savings, emergency funds, and debt repayment. **This is very important.** Aim to save at least 10-20% of your income and allocate additional funds towards paying off high-interest debt.

Consider using the 50/30/20 rule as a guideline for budgeting. Allocate 50% of your income towards needs, 30% towards wants, and 20% towards savings and debt repayment. Adjust the percentages based on your individual financial situation and goals.

Regularly monitor your budget and review your spending habits to identify areas where adjustments can be made. Track your progress towards financial goals and make necessary changes to your budget as needed.

Anticipate irregular expenses such as car repairs, medical bills, or holiday spending by setting aside funds in a separate savings account. Planning for these expenses in advance helps prevent financial stress when they arise.

HOW TO AVOID IMPULSIVE SPENDING

The next thing we should discuss in-depth is how to ensure you're not compulsively spending. There are strategies you can implement that'll help you avoid impulsive spending and staying on budget. Here are some I suggest for you:

Create a Spending Plan:

When creating a spending plan, list all sources of income and categorize expenses into fixed and variable categories. Allocate specific amounts to each category, ensuring that essential expenses are prioritized. Regularly review and adjust the spending plan as needed to reflect changes in income or expenses.

Identify Spending Impulse:

Take time to reflect on personal triggers for impulsive spending, such as emotional stress or environmental cues like advertisements. Once identified, develop coping strategies to address these triggers, such as practicing mindfulness or finding alternative ways to manage stress.

Practice Mindful Spending:

Before making a purchase, pause and ask yourself whether the item is a necessity or a discretionary want. Consider how the purchase aligns with your financial goals and whether it provides long-term value. By practicing mindfulness, you can make more intentional spending decisions.

Implement a Waiting Period:

When tempted to make an impulsive purchase, commit to waiting a set amount of time, such as 24 hours, before completing the transaction. During this waiting period, reassess whether the purchase is truly necessary or if it was driven by impulse. This delay can help prevent rash decisions and promote more thoughtful spending.

Set Spending Limits:

Determine spending limits for discretionary categories based on your budgetary constraints and financial goals. Use tools like budgeting apps or spreadsheets to track spending in real-time and stay within these limits. Adjust spending as necessary to ensure alignment with your financial plan.

Use Cash Instead of Cards:

Consider using cash or a debit card for discretionary purchases to create a tangible connection between spending and available funds. When using cash, you can physically see the money leaving your wallet, which may deter impulsive spending. Additionally, using a debit card limits spending to available funds, reducing the risk of overspending on credit.

Track Spending Regularly:

Make it a habit to review your spending regularly, preferably on a weekly or monthly basis. Use budgeting tools or apps to categorize expenses and identify areas where spending can be reduced or redirected towards savings goals. Regular monitoring helps maintain awareness of your financial habits and progress towards your goals.

Avoid Temptations:

Minimize exposure to situations or environments that may trigger impulsive spending. Unsubscribe from marketing emails, limit time spent browsing online shopping sites, and avoid visiting retail stores unnecessarily. By reducing exposure to temptations, you can decrease the likelihood of impulsive purchases.

Focus on Long-Term Goals:

Keep your long-term financial goals at the forefront of your mind when making spending decisions. Visualize the benefits of staying on budget, such as achieving financial freedom, paying off debt, or saving for important milestones. By maintaining focus on your overarching goals, you can prioritize spending in alignment with your priorities.

USING DIGITAL TOOLS FOR ORGANIZING AND PLANNING

By utilizing digital tools and apps for financial organization and planning, you can streamline the budgeting process, gain better insights into your spending habits, and make more informed decisions about your finances.

These tools can empower you to take control of your financial future and work towards achieving your goals with confidence. Here is everything you need in 9 steps:

1. Research and Choose the Right App:

Begin by researching different financial management apps available on the market. Look for apps that offer features aligned with your specific needs, such as budget tracking, expense categorization, bill reminders, and goal setting. Consider factors like user interface, security features, and compatibility with your devices before making a decision.

2. Set Up Accounts and Link Financial Institutions:

Once you've chosen an app, set up accounts and link your financial institutions, including checking accounts, savings accounts, credit cards, and investment accounts.

Many financial apps offer secure connections to banks and other financial institutions, allowing for automatic data syncing and real-time updates on account balances and transactions.

3. Create a Budget and Set Financial Goals:

Use the app's budgeting features to create a personalized budget based on your income, expenses, and financial goals.

Set spending limits for different categories, track progress towards your goals, and receive alerts or notifications when you exceed budgeted amounts.

Establish short-term and long-term financial goals, such as saving for a vacation, paying off debt, or building an emergency fund, and use the app to track your progress over time.

4. Track Expenses and Categorize Transactions:

Regularly monitor your spending by categorizing transactions and expenses within the app.

Assign categories such as groceries, dining out, entertainment, utilities, and transportation to each transaction to gain insights into your spending habits and identify areas where you can cut costs or redirect funds towards savings goals.

Many apps offer customizable spending categories and allow for easy categorization of transactions with just a few taps.

5. Set Up Bill Reminders and Alerts:

Take advantage of the app's bill reminder and alert features to stay on top of recurring expenses, such as rent, utilities, subscriptions, and loan payments. Set up reminders for upcoming due dates, receive alerts for upcoming bills, and track payment history to avoid late fees and penalties. Some apps even offer automatic bill pay options, allowing you to schedule payments directly from the app.

6. Monitor Net Worth and Financial Trends:

Use the app to track your net worth and monitor changes in your financial position over time. View detailed reports and charts showing income, expenses, savings, investments, and debt to gain a comprehensive understanding of your financial health.

Identify trends and patterns in your spending and saving behavior to make informed decisions about future financial planning.

7. Sync across Devices and Share with Family Members:

Choose an app that offers multi-device syncing capabilities, allowing you to access your financial information from anywhere, anytime.

Sync accounts across smartphones, tablets, and computers to ensure consistent and up-to-date data across all devices. Some apps also offer sharing features, allowing you to collaborate with family members or partners on budgeting and financial goals.

9. Review and Adjust Regularly:

Schedule regular reviews of your financial information within the app to track progress towards your goals and identify areas for improvement.

Use reports, charts, and budgeting tools to analyze spending patterns, identify trends, and make adjustments to your budget as needed. Stay proactive in managing your finances and make informed decisions based on your financial data.

Chapter 9

Workplace Strategies

Advocating for accommodations in the workplace, if applicable, is essential, to ensure you can perform your job duties effectively and thrive in a professional environment. Before advocating for accommodation in your workplace, you need to put some things into place first.

Know Your Rights:

Familiarize yourself with relevant laws and regulations that protect individuals with disabilities, such as the Americans with Disabilities Act (ADA) in the United States or similar legislation in other countries. Understand your rights to reasonable accommodations in the workplace and how they apply to your specific situation.

Understand Your Needs:

Identify specific challenges or barriers related to your ADHD symptoms that impact your performance at work. Reflect on accommodations or adjustments that could address these challenges and support your success in the workplace. Common accommodations for ADHD may include flexible work hours, ergonomic workspace arrangements, or assistive technology.

Gather Relevant Documentation:

Obtain documentation from healthcare professionals or qualified specialists that support your need for accommodations in the workplace.

This may include medical records, diagnostic assessments, or letters from healthcare providers detailing your ADHD diagnosis and recommended accommodations. Having documented evidence strengthens your case when requesting accommodations from your employer.

Initiate a Conversation with Your Employer:

Schedule a meeting with your supervisor or human resources representative to discuss your ADHD diagnosis and the accommodations you are requesting.

Approach the conversation with professionalism and transparency, emphasizing your commitment to your job and your desire to perform at your best with the appropriate support.

Propose Specific Accommodations:

Clearly articulate the accommodations you are requesting and explain how they would address your specific needs and enhance your productivity and performance. Provide examples of how similar accommodations have been successful in other workplaces or industries.

Highlight the Benefits for the Employer:

Emphasize the benefits of providing accommodations for both you and your employer. Accommodations can lead to increased productivity, improved job satisfaction, reduced absenteeism, and enhanced retention of valuable employees. Frame accommodations as an investment in your success and the overall success of the organization.

Collaborate on Implementation:

Work collaboratively with your employer to develop a plan for implementing the requested accommodations. Be open to suggestions and feedback from your employer, and explore creative solutions to address your needs while considering the practicalities of your work environment.

Educate Colleagues and Supervisors:

Take the opportunity to educate colleagues and supervisors about ADHD and the accommodations you are receiving. Foster a supportive and inclusive work environment by promoting awareness and understanding of neurodiversity in the workplace.

HOW TO MANAGING WORKLOAD

- **Prioritize Tasks:** Start by identifying tasks and projects based on their urgency and importance. Use prioritization techniques such as the Eisenhower Matrix or ABC prioritization to categorize tasks into "urgent and important," "important but not urgent," "urgent but not important," and "neither urgent nor important." Focus your attention and energy on high-priority tasks first.

- **Set Realistic Deadlines:** Establish realistic deadlines for completing tasks and projects. Avoid overcommitting or underestimating the time required to complete tasks. Break down larger goals into smaller milestones with achievable deadlines to maintain momentum and track progress effectively.

- **Utilize Digital Tools and Apps:** Take advantage of digital tools and apps designed to help manage workload and deadlines. Use task management apps like Todoist, Trello, or Asana to create to-do lists, set deadlines, and track progress on tasks and projects. Calendar apps like Google Calendar or Microsoft Outlook can help schedule appointments, meetings, and deadlines.

- **Create Daily and Weekly Plans:** Start each day by creating a prioritized to-do list or plan outlining tasks to be completed. Review and update your plan regularly throughout the day as priorities shift or new tasks arise. At the end of each week, evaluate your progress, celebrate accomplishments, and adjust plans for the following week as needed.

- **Implement the Two-Minute Rule:** Apply the two-minute rule to quickly complete small tasks or action items that can be done in two minutes or less. This rule helps prevent procrastination and reduces the accumulation of minor tasks that can contribute to feelings of overwhelm.

- **Minimize Distractions:** Identify and minimize distractions in your work environment to maintain focus and productivity. Use strategies such as creating a dedicated workspace, turning off notifications, using noise-cancelling headphones, or implementing website blockers to limit distractions from email, social media, or other sources.

- **Delegate Tasks When Possible:** Recognize when tasks can be delegated to colleagues or team members and leverage their skills and expertise to lighten your workload. Delegating tasks allows you to focus on higher-priority responsibilities and increases overall efficiency within the team.

COMMUNICATING OPENLY WITH SUPERVISORS ABOUT ADHD-RELATED CHALLENGES

Communicating openly with supervisors or colleagues about ADHD-related challenges is crucial for fostering understanding, support, and collaboration in the workplace.

This will ultimately create a more inclusive and accommodating work environment. To increase your chances of being heard, you need to do 9 simple things. Here are they:

1. **Do Your Homework:** Take the time to educate yourself about ADHD, including its symptoms, challenges, and how it may impact job performance. Understand your rights and protections under relevant laws, such as the Americans with Disabilities Act (ADA) or similar legislation in your country.

2. **Choose the Right Time and Place:** Select an appropriate time and setting to have the conversation with your supervisor or colleagues. Choose a private and neutral environment where you can speak openly without interruptions. Avoid discussing sensitive topics in high-stress or time-sensitive situations.

3. **Prepare Talking Points:** Prepare talking points or an agenda for the conversation to ensure you cover key points effectively. Outline specific ADHD-related challenges you are experiencing in the

workplace and how they impact your performance. Be clear and concise in your communication.

4. **Be Honest and Transparent:** Approach the conversation with honesty and transparency about your ADHD diagnosis and how it affects you professionally. Share personal experiences or examples to help others understand the challenges you face. Express your commitment to finding solutions and improving your performance.

5. **Focus on Solutions:** Shift the focus of the conversation from problems to potential solutions. Propose specific accommodations or adjustments that could help mitigate ADHD-related challenges in the workplace. Offer ideas for how colleagues or supervisors can support you in achieving your job responsibilities effectively.

6. **Ask for Support and Understanding:** Clearly communicate your need for support and understanding from supervisors and colleagues. Emphasize that ADHD is a legitimate neurodevelopmental condition that may require accommodations or adjustments to optimize your performance. Request feedback on how they can best support you in your role.

7. **Listen and Validate Concerns:** Be receptive to feedback and concerns raised by supervisors or colleagues during the conversation. Listen actively and validate their perspectives while also advocating for your own needs. Foster an open dialogue where both parties feel heard and respected.

8. **Address Misconceptions or Stigma:** Take the opportunity to dispel misconceptions or stigma

surrounding ADHD in the workplace. Provide accurate information about the condition and its impact on individuals' functioning. Advocate for greater awareness and acceptance of neurodiversity in the workplace.

9. **Follow Up and Maintain Communication:** After the initial conversation, follow up with supervisors or colleagues to ensure ongoing communication and support. Keep them informed of any changes in your needs or circumstances related to ADHD, and collaborate on strategies for addressing challenges as they arise.

CAREER PATH

Exploring career paths and environments that align with individual strengths and preferences is essential if you want to thrive professionally and find fulfillment in your work.

Begin by conducting a thorough self-assessment to identify your strengths, interests, values, and preferences. Reflect on past experiences, hobbies, and activities that have energized and engaged you.

Consider your natural talents, skills, and areas of expertise that you enjoy utilizing in your work.

Once you do that, explore a wide range of career options and industries that align with your strengths and interests.

Use online resources such as career assessment tools, job search websites, and professional networking platforms to research different career paths and learn about job requirements, qualifications, and growth opportunities.

Now, it's time to reach out to mentors, career counselors, or professionals in fields of interest for guidance and advice. Connect with individuals who have experience or expertise in industries or roles you're considering and learn from their insights and experiences. Seek mentorship to gain valuable perspective and guidance on navigating career decisions.

Before taking any job offer, evaluate different work environments and organizational cultures to identify those that resonate with your preferences and needs.

Consider factors such as company size, structure, flexibility, and company values when exploring potential employers.

Seek environments that offer flexibility, autonomy, and opportunities for creativity and innovation.

Don't just stick with old methods of job searching. Consider non-traditional or alternative career paths that may offer flexibility and opportunities for leveraging your strengths. Explore freelance work, entrepreneurship, remote work, or gig economy opportunities that align with your skills and interests. Embrace flexibility and adaptability in exploring diverse career options.

Networking can also boost your chances, especially if you know your way around. Find a way to network with professionals in your industries of interest and conduct informational interviews to learn more about different career paths.

Reach out to professionals via professional networking platforms, alumni networks, or industry events to request informational interviews. Use these conversations to gather insights, ask questions, and expand your network.

Don't be shy to seek opportunities to gain relevant experience and skills in industries or roles of interest.

Consider internships, volunteer work, part-time roles, or freelance projects to build your resume and explore different career paths. Look for opportunities to apply your strengths and interests in real-world settings and gain valuable experience.

Don't forget to commit to lifelong learning and professional development to enhance your skills and stay competitive in your chosen field.

Pursue relevant certifications, courses, or training programs to deepen your expertise and expand your skill set. Stay abreast of industry trends, developments, and emerging technologies to remain agile and adaptable in your career.

Regularly assess job fit and satisfaction in your current role or career path. Pay attention to factors such as job satisfaction, work-life balance, alignment with values, and opportunities for growth and advancement. Be willing to reassess and pivot if you find that your current career path no longer aligns with your strengths and preferences.

Chapter 10

Communication Skills

Effective Communication with Peers

When discussing with peers, practice active listening when engaging with peers. Give your full attention to the speaker, maintain eye contact, and avoid interrupting. Demonstrate understanding by paraphrasing what you've heard and asking clarifying questions to ensure clear comprehension.

Show empathy and understanding towards your peers' perspectives and experiences. Validate their feelings and viewpoints, even if you disagree. Avoid judgment and strive to create a supportive and inclusive communication environment.

Be willing to share your experiences, concerns, and feedback with peers, and encourage them to do the same. Transparency promotes trust and strengthens relationships.

Treat your peers with respect and courtesy in all communication interactions. Use polite language, avoid sarcasm or derogatory remarks, and show appreciation for their contributions and perspectives. Cultivate a positive and respectful communication climate that fosters mutual respect and dignity.

Develop effective conflict resolution skills to address disagreements or misunderstandings that may arise with peers. When resolving conflicts, remain calm and composed and focus on finding mutually beneficial solutions. Use "I" statements to express your feelings and concerns without blaming or accusing others.

Finally, approach challenges or obstacles collaboratively with peers by brainstorming solutions and leveraging collective expertise. Encourage open dialogue and creative thinking to generate innovative solutions to shared problems. Foster a culture of teamwork and cooperation to achieve common goals.

Effective Communication with Family

Allocate dedicated time for family communication without distractions. Schedule regular family meetings or bonding activities where everyone can participate and engage in open dialogue without interruptions from external factors.

Share personal updates, achievements, and highlights with family members to maintain strong connections and foster a sense of closeness. Celebrate each other's successes, milestones, and accomplishments to strengthen family bonds and build a positive communication climate.

Respect each family member's boundaries, preferences, and differences in communication styles. Avoid imposing your opinions or expectations onto others and strive to understand and appreciate their unique perspectives and preferences. Create a safe space where everyone feels comfortable expressing themselves authentically.

Express appreciation, gratitude, and affection towards family members regularly to reinforce positive communication and strengthen emotional bonds. Show appreciation for each other's contributions, support, and efforts to nurture a culture of love and appreciation within the family.

Be patient and understanding when communicating with family members, especially during challenging or stressful situations. Practice empathy and compassion, and be willing to offer support and assistance when needed. Cultivate an atmosphere of patience and understanding to promote harmonious family relationships.

Effective Communication with Coworkers

Prioritize professionalism in all communication interactions with coworkers. Use formal language, adhere to workplace norms and etiquette, and maintain a respectful and courteous demeanor at all times.

Avoid personal topics or discussions unrelated to work to ensure a professional communication environment.

Clarify expectations and responsibilities with coworkers to ensure alignment and prevent misunderstandings. Clearly communicate project objectives, timelines, and deliverables, and discuss individual roles and contributions within the team. Establish clear channels for feedback and accountability to promote transparency and efficiency.

Foster effective collaboration with coworkers by promoting open communication, sharing information, and soliciting input from team members. Encourage brainstorming sessions, collaborative problem-solving, and knowledge sharing to leverage collective expertise and creativity. Cultivate a culture of teamwork and cooperation to achieve shared objectives.

Practice empathy when interacting with coworkers to foster understanding and build rapport. Listen attentively to their perspectives, concerns, and ideas, and demonstrate empathy by acknowledging their feelings and validating their experiences. Show genuine interest in their contributions and experiences to strengthen professional relationships.

Provide constructive feedback to coworkers in a respectful and constructive manner to support their growth and development. Offer feedback that is specific, actionable, and focused on performance improvement, while also highlighting strengths and areas for development. Foster a culture of continuous feedback and learning within the team.

Adapt your communication style to suit the preferences and needs of different coworkers. Tailor your approach based on individual communication styles, personalities, and preferences to enhance understanding and rapport. Be flexible and adaptable in your communication to accommodate diverse perspectives and work styles.

Expressing Needs and Setting Boundaries

Assertive communication is crucial for expressing needs and setting boundaries effectively in personal and professional relationships. And it's simple to do, all it requires is a little attention to a few things:

- **Use "I" Statements:** Start statements with "I" to express feelings, thoughts, and needs directly without blaming or accusing others. For example, say "I feel overwhelmed when I have too many tasks assigned at once" instead of "You always give me too much work."

- **Be Clear and Specific:** Clearly articulate your needs and boundaries in a direct and specific manner. Avoid ambiguity or vagueness by providing concrete examples and explanations. State what you need or expect from others explicitly to avoid misunderstandings.

- **Set Clear Consequences:** Establish clear consequences for respecting or violating boundaries to reinforce assertive communication. Communicate boundaries assertively and assertively enforce consequences if boundaries are disregarded. Consistency is key to maintaining boundaries effectively.

- **Use Assertive Body Language:** Pay attention to your body language when expressing needs and setting boundaries. Stand or sit upright, maintain eye contact, and use confident gestures to convey assertiveness. Avoid crossing arms or appearing defensive, which can undermine your message.

- **Practice Self-Advocacy:** Advocate for your needs and rights assertively without apologizing or downplaying your importance. Recognize your worth and assert your right to set boundaries and prioritize self-care. Assertiveness is not selfish; it's essential for maintaining healthy relationships and well-being.

- **Practice Assertive Scripts:** Prepare assertive scripts or phrases in advance for challenging situations where you need to express your needs or set boundaries. Rehearse these scripts to build confidence and clarity in communicating assertively. Use assertive language to assert your position confidently and respectfully.

- **Use Assertive Tone and Language:** Pay attention to your tone of voice and language when expressing needs and setting boundaries. Speak in a calm, firm tone and use assertive language that conveys confidence and respect. Avoid aggressive or passive language that may escalate conflicts or undermine your message.

TIPS FOR ACTIVE LISTENING

Give Your Full Attention:

Focus your attention fully on the speaker and minimize distractions to ensure active listening. Put away electronic devices, avoid multitasking, and maintain eye contact with the speaker to signal your engagement and attentiveness.

Show Interest and Empathy:

Demonstrate genuine interest and empathy towards the speaker's message to encourage open communication. Use nonverbal cues such as nodding, smiling, and leaning forward to convey attentiveness and understanding. Reflect the speaker's emotions and validate their feelings to foster a supportive communication environment.

Use Verbal and Nonverbal Affirmations:

Use verbal affirmations such as "I see," "I understand," or "That makes sense" to acknowledge the speaker's message and encourage further dialogue. Employ nonverbal cues such as nodding, mirroring, and maintaining an open body posture to convey active listening and engagement.

Ask Clarifying Questions:

Ask clarifying questions to ensure clear understanding and encourage the speaker to elaborate on key points.

Paraphrase or summarize the speaker's message to confirm comprehension and demonstrate active engagement. Clarifying questions demonstrate genuine interest and promote deeper understanding of the topic.

Avoid Interrupting:

Refrain from interrupting the speaker or interjecting with your own thoughts or opinions while they are speaking. Practice patience and restraint, allowing the speaker to express themselves fully before offering your perspective. Interrupting can disrupt the flow of conversation and hinder effective communication.

Focus on Nonverbal Cues:

Pay attention to the speaker's nonverbal cues, such as facial expressions, tone of voice, and body language, to gain insight into their emotions and intentions. Notice subtle cues that may convey underlying feelings or attitudes and adjust your response accordingly. Nonverbal cues provide valuable context for understanding the speaker's message.

Conclusion

As we wrap up our journey through this book, it's important to acknowledge the significant strides you've made in exploring strategies to effectively manage ADHD symptoms and enhance your daily functioning.

The journey towards better self-management is both challenging and rewarding, and your commitment to seeking solutions is commendable.

You have the power to take control of your ADHD symptoms and improve your daily functioning.

Embrace your strengths, recognize your potential, and believe in your ability to overcome challenges.

You are not defined by your ADHD; rather, it is a part of who you are, and you have the capacity to thrive despite it.

Take ownership of your journey towards self-improvement and advocate for your needs.

Use the strategies outlined in this resource as tools to navigate life's challenges and achieve your goals.

Empower yourself to make positive changes, cultivate resilience, and live life on your own terms.

Implementing the strategies outlined in this resource consistently is key to achieving lasting results and overcoming the challenges associated with ADHD.

Consistency breeds habit, and habits shape behavior over time.

By incorporating these strategies into your daily routine and making them a part of your lifestyle, you can experience meaningful improvements in various aspects of your life.

Consistency is not always easy, and setbacks may occur along the way.

However, it's important to remain resilient and maintain a positive outlook.

Each step forward, no matter how small, is a step towards progress and growth. Celebrate your successes and learn from your setbacks, knowing that every effort contributes to your well-being.

Remember that change takes time, and patience is key.

Be kind to yourself as you navigate this journey, and don't hesitate to seek support from loved ones, healthcare professionals, or support groups when needed.

You are not alone in this journey, and there is strength in seeking assistance and sharing experiences with others who understand.

Recommended Resources

If you're interested in further exploring strategies and resources for managing ADHD, here are some recommended books and websites:

Books:

"Driven to Distraction: Recognizing and Coping with Attention Deficit Disorder" by Edward M. Hallowell and John J. Ratey

"Delivered from Distraction: Getting the Most out of Life with Attention Deficit Disorder" by Edward M. Hallowell and John J. Ratey

"Taking Charge of Adult ADHD" by Russell A. Barkley

"The ADHD Effect on Marriage: Understand and Rebuild Your Relationship in Six Steps" by Melissa Orlov

"Smart but Stuck: Emotions in Teens and Adults with ADHD" by Thomas E. Brown

Websites:

CHADD (Children and Adults with Attention-Deficit/Hyperactivity Disorder): A nonprofit organization providing education, advocacy, and support for individuals with ADHD and their families. Website: chadd.org

ADDitude Magazine: An online resource providing articles, webinars, expert advice, and community forums for individuals affected by ADHD. Website: additudemag.com

Understood: A website offering resources, tools, and support for individuals with learning and attention issues, including ADHD. Website: understood.org

National Institute of Mental Health (NIMH): The NIMH offers information and research updates on ADHD, including treatment options and clinical trials. Website: nimh.nih.gov/health/topics/attention-deficit-hyperactivity-disorder-adhd/index.shtml

Online Communities and Support Groups:

Joining online communities and support groups can provide valuable peer support, advice, and shared experiences. Websites like Reddit (r/ADHD), Facebook groups, and local meetup groups can be excellent resources for connecting with others affected by ADHD.

Educational Workshops and Seminars:

Many organizations, clinics, and mental health centers offer workshops, seminars, and webinars on ADHD management, coping skills, and strategies for success. Check local listings or online event calendars for upcoming educational events in your area.

These resources can provide additional insights, support, and guidance for individuals seeking to better understand and manage ADHD in their lives. It's important to explore various resources and find the ones that resonate most with your individual needs and preferences.

Videos and Webinars:

Websites like YouTube and TED Talks offer a variety of videos and webinars featuring experts discussing ADHD-related topics, coping strategies, and personal stories. Search for reputable channels or organizations specializing in ADHD education and advocacy.

Podcasts:

Podcasts can be a convenient and informative way to learn about ADHD while on the go. Look for podcasts hosted by psychologists, educators, or individuals with lived experience of ADHD. Some recommended podcasts include "ADHD Experts Podcast" by ADDitude Magazine and "ADHD reWired" by Eric Tivers.

Workbooks and Worksheets:

Workbooks and worksheets designed for ADHD can provide practical exercises, tools, and activities for managing symptoms and improving daily functioning. "The ADHD Workbook for Teens" by Lara Honos-Webb and "The ADHD Workbook for Kids" by Lawrence Shapiro are examples of helpful resources.

Online Courses:

Many online platforms offer courses specifically focused on ADHD management, executive functioning skills, and strategies for success. Websites like Udemy, Coursera, and Skillshare may have courses taught by professionals specializing in ADHD.

Apps and Digital Tools:

Mobile apps and digital tools can be valuable resources for managing ADHD symptoms, organizing tasks, and improving productivity. Look for apps that offer features such as task lists, reminders, time tracking, and mood tracking. Examples include Todoist, Trello, Forest, and Headspace.